Make Room for the Mystery of God

Visit of John Paul II to the USA 1995

ST. PAUL BOOKS & MEDIA

BOSTON

ISBN 0-8198-4783-6

Cover photo: Arturo Mari

Printed and published by Pauline Books & Media, 50 St. Paul's Avenue, Boston, MA 02130.

Pauline Books & Media is the publishing house of the Daughters of St. Paul, an international congregation of women religious serving the Church with the communications media.

1 2 3 4 5   99 98 97 96 95

America has a reputation the world over, a reputation of power, prestige and wealth. But not everyone here is powerful; not everyone here is rich. In fact, America's sometimes extravagant affluence often conceals much hardship and poverty.

In the midst of the magnificent scientific and technological civilization of which America is proud...is there room for the mystery of God?

Contents

Arrival at
Newark International Airport

Greetings to the President, Church leaders and the American people at Newark International Airport, October 4, 1995

Mr. President, dear friends, dear people of America,

It is a great joy for me to return to the United States, as I had hoped to do last year. Thank you all for receiving me so warmly. This is a land of much generosity, and its people have always been quick to extend their hands in friendship and to offer hospitality. Thank you especially, President Clinton, for coming here today in that same spirit.

For my part, I greet you and all the representatives of the federal, state and local governments. I greet the bishops' conference of the United States and the individual bishops who have invited me to their dioceses and have worked so hard, with countless co-workers, to prepare for this visit. I look forward to meeting the Catholic communities of Newark, Brooklyn, New York and Baltimore, as well as our brothers and sisters of other Christian churches and ecclesial communities. To the members of the Jewish faith I extend a very cordial greeting and my respectful best wishes on this day of special significance for them.

I greet all the people of this great nation, of every race, color, creed and social condition. I pray for you all and assure you of my profound esteem.

I too come as a pilgrim of peace and understanding among peoples.

Exactly thirty years ago today my predecessor, Pope Paul VI, spoke to the United Nations General Assembly and delivered a message that still resounds in many hearts. "No more war, war never again!" He went on to appeal: "Peace, it is peace which must guide the destinies of people" (Pope Paul VI, Address to U. N. General Assembly, October 4, 1965).

I too come as a pilgrim of peace and understanding among peoples. Tomorrow, in observance of the United Nations' 50th anniversary, I shall return there to express my deep conviction that the ideals and intentions which gave origin to that worldwide organization half a century ago are more indispensable than ever in a world searching for purpose.

The world, in fact, is undergoing a profound transformation. Opportunities for justice, reconciliation and development are visible in parts of the world where they were hardly discernible even a few years ago—almost within our reach, it seems, but still so difficult to grasp. Ancient rivalries and suspicions still compromise the cause of peace. We must find ways to set them aside. If we do not, history and the Lord of history will judge us harshly.

Especially since the events of 1989, the role of the United States in the world has taken on a new prominence. Your widespread influence is at once political, economic, military and, due to your communications media, cultural. It is vital for the human family that in continuing to seek advancement in many different fields—science, business, education and art, and wherever else your creativity leads you—America keeps compassion, generosity and concern for others at the very heart of its efforts.

In particular, for nations and peoples emerging from a long period of trial, your country stands upon the world scene as a model of a democratic society at an advanced stage of development. Your power of example carries with it heavy responsibilities. Use it well, America! Be an example of justice and civic virtue, freedom fulfilled in goodness, at home and abroad!

From its beginning until now, the United States has been a haven for generation after generation of new arrivals. Men, women and children have streamed here from every corner of the globe, building new lives and forming a society of rich ethnic and racial diversity, based on a commitment to a shared vision of human dignity and freedom. Of the United States we can truly say, *E pluribus unum.*

It is my prayerful hope that America will persevere in its own best traditions of openness and opportunity. It would indeed be sad if the United States were to turn away from that enterprising spirit which has always sought the most practical and responsible ways of continuing to share with others the blessings God has richly bestowed here.

America will continue to be a land of promise as long as it remains a land of freedom and justice for all.

The same spirit of creative generosity will help you to meet the needs of your own poor and disadvantaged. They too have a role to play in building a society truly worthy of the human person—a society in which none are so poor that they have nothing to give and none are so rich that they have nothing to receive. The poor have needs which are not only material and economic, but also involve liberating their potential to work out their own destiny and to provide for the well-being of their families and communities. America will continue to be a land of promise as long as it remains a land of freedom and justice for all.

Mr. President, ladies and gentlemen: I come as one who has an abiding hope in America's noble destiny. I thank God for allowing me to return to you again. Thank you and God bless you all!

Sacred Heart Cathedral, Newark, New Jersey

Address to the clergy, seminarians, religious and laity at Sacred Heart Cathedral, October 4, 1995

Dear Archbishop McCarrick, and my other brother bishops, dear brother priests, dear seminarians, men and women religious, and Lay faithful of the family of God which is the Church in Newark!

We are gathered in this cathedral dedicated to the Sacred Heart of Jesus in order to give thanks to the most blessed Trinity for the bonds of faith and love which unite us in the one, holy, catholic and apostolic Church. The presence of the President of the United States at this evening prayer helps us call to mind that it is precisely our service of God which inspires and motivates the healthy pride which we all feel in our native land. This evening let us thank God for the extraordinary human epic that is the United States of America.

This magnificent building stands in the heart of Newark as a powerful reminder of God's steadfast love for his people and as a sign of faith in Christ, our "hope of glory" (Col 1:27). The cathedral made of stone is the symbol of the living Church, "God's household" (1 Tim 3:15), which is open to everyone without exception, to men and women "of every race and tongue, of every people and nation" (Rev 5:9). You—the people of God in Newark and throughout New Jersey—are the "living stones" (1 Pet 2:5) which make up the body of Christ in the midst of your city and state. Wherever you are—in your families, neighborhoods, places of work or recreation—you are called to build up the Church in faith, hope and love.

The Church is alive in you! God, who is the master builder of his holy temple, has poured his love into your hearts through the Holy Spirit (cf. Rom 5:5)! You have received the gift of new life. You have been charged with bringing the good news "to all creation" (Mk 16:15).

The stirring challenge of the new evangelization—the aim of which is to proclaim that Jesus Christ is the center of history, the hope of humanity and the joy of every heart (cf. *Gaudium et Spes*, n. 45)—was faced by last year's archdiocesan synod. I greet with affection all of you who so zealously took part as delegates in that important assembly. The synod wisely called for a great mobilization of resources so that all Catholics would receive the solid spiritual and doctrinal formation needed in order to bear convincing witness to their faith and assume their full role in the Church's mission. I pray that, as a result of the synod, the Archdiocese of Newark will become ever more "of one heart and one mind" (Acts 4:32)—a community joyously united with its bishops and priests in attentively listening to the word of

God, devoutly celebrating the sacraments, and generously meeting the needs of others.

The new evangelization of America calls for a great spiritual maturity.

With special affection I greet my brothers in the priesthood, and thank each one of you for your dedicated service of the Gospel! The Lord has chosen you to be "in the forefront" in bringing souls to him *(Pastores Dabo Vobis*, n. 27). Like Christ, the head and shepherd of the Church, you must know, tend and offer your life for your flock (cf. Jn 10:11-16). Ordination configures you to Christ the servant—to him who humbly washed his apostles' feet because he came among us "not to be served but to serve" (cf. Mk 10:45). Such selfless service is the model of all ministry in the Church. As you return to your parishes or to the various apostolates in which you are engaged, I pray that—in the words of St. Paul— God will make you "worthy of his call, and fulfill by his power every honest intention and work of faith" (2 Thes 1:11).

To the seminarians—and how heartening it is to know that your number is increasing!—I offer a special word of encouragement. The new evangelization of America calls for a great spiritual maturity on your part. The gift of the priesthood demands that you follow Christ "even unto death on a cross" (cf. Phil 2:8). Without the virtues of self-discipline, diligent contemplation of the truth, simplicity of life and joyful dedication to others you will not have the inner strength to combat the culture of death which is threatening the modern world. I urge you to pray each day: "O good Jesus, make me a priest like unto your own heart." Christ himself is your inheritance (cf. Ps 16:5-6). He will never abandon you or disappoint you!

With profound gratitude for your immense contribution to the Church's life, I embrace all the men and women religious. Whether "your life is hidden with Christ in God" (cf. Col 3:3) in solitude, penance and contemplation, or whether you are actively engaged in the world, the whole ecclesial community looks to you to see what it means to love the Lord with an undivided heart. The recognition of the "genius of woman" and of the specifically feminine charisms which women religious bring to the Church's life and mission is a providential sign of our times. If in the past these gifts were sometimes insufficiently esteemed or thwarted in their legitimate expression, now is the time for all of us to work together to follow where the Lord leads, in love and fidelity. May the Holy Spirit "strengthen your hearts, making them blameless and holy before our God and Father" (1 Thes 3:13), so that you may serve his people with ever greater joy!

To the whole Church in Newark and New Jersey I repeat the words of encouragement found in the First Letter of Peter: "There is cause for rejoicing here...because you are achieving faith's goal, your salvation" (1 Pet 1:6, 9).

Dear friends in Christ, the First Letter of Peter exhorts us to be clothed with humility in our dealings with one another. We read: "Bow humbly under God's mighty hand, so that in due time he may lift you high"

(5:6). This lowliness and humility is explained as abandoning ourselves into the hands of God: "Cast all your cares on him because he cares for you" (5:7). Yes, God holds humanity in the highest esteem! God reveres everything that is authentically human—everything that affects individuals and societies, nations and states!

The powerful and the mighty ought to show meekness in their dealings with the weak.

As you well know, I have come to the United States in connection with the 50th anniversary of the founding of the United Nations. That organization exists to serve the common good of the human family, and therefore it is fitting that the Pope speak there as a witness to the hope of the Gospel (cf. Col 1:23). The United Nations is an instrument of dialogue and peace. The criteria of its actions ought always to be the integral well-being of people. The challenge which is permanently before its member states, agencies and personnel is similar to the challenge which confronts every individual: "In your relations with one another clothe yourselves with humility" (1 Pet 5:5). In particular, the powerful and the mighty ought to show meekness in their dealings with the weak. The powerful always need to remember that they owe their position to God—to the one who "is stern with the arrogant but who shows kindness to the humble" (1 Pet 5:5). Nations and governments—like individuals—need to acknowledge that the Lord "rules the world with justice; with fairness he rules the peoples and guides the nations" (Ps 67:5-6).

The First Letter of Peter also recalls the need for watchfulness: "Stay sober and alert" (5:8). Fifty years ago, after the end of the incredible destruction caused by the Second World War, the United Nations organization was established as an international forum of vigilance at the service of peace and justice in the world. The United Nations has a necessary role to play in preventing and relieving the enormous sufferings which the world's peoples and nations inflict on each other. In the 20th century these sufferings have reached unprecedented proportions in wars and conflicts, and in political and ideological oppression caused by the greed and arrogance of those who plot evil in their hearts.

The history of the world in the last fifty years cannot be written without reference to the United Nations. Is it not still needed, to watch and warn and exhort when conflict and injustice threaten the tranquillity of order? Should it not be strengthened as the guarantor of peace, justice and humanitarian concern whether in the Balkans, in Africa or in any place where these values are threatened? Should it not be reformed to ensure that it will be guided by an objective assessment of the international situation, in order to be a credible forum in which to address issues of fundamental importance for the building of a more human and just world?

Our prayer for peace is therefore also a prayer for the United Nations organization. St. Francis of Assisi, whose feast we celebrate today, shines forth as a great lover and artisan of peace. Let us invoke his intercession upon the United Nations' work for justice and peace throughout the world.

May the God of all grace, who has called us to everlasting glory in Christ, confirm and strengthen all who work and suffer for the peace and well-being of the human family. He alone is the Lord of life and history. To him we pray:

O God, be gracious and bless us
and let your face shed its light upon us.
So will your ways be known upon earth
and all nations learn your saving help (Ps 67:2-3).

To him we commend the Church in the United States, and the local Church of Newark and the surrounding dioceses. To him be honor, glory and praise! Amen.

The U.N. General Assembly

An address given to the General Assembly of the United Nations, October 5, 1995

Mr. President, Ladies and Gentlemen,

It is an honor for me to have the opportunity to address this international assembly and to join the men and women of every country, race, language and culture in celebrating the 50th anniversary of the founding of the United Nations Organization. In coming before this distinguished assembly, I am vividly aware that through you I am in some way addressing the whole family of peoples living on the face of the earth. My words are meant as a sign of the interest and esteem of the Apostolic See and of the Catholic Church for this institution. They echo the voices of all those who see in the United Nations the hope of a better future for human society.

I wish to express my heartfelt gratitude in the first place to the secretary general, Dr. Boutros Boutros-Ghali, for having warmly encouraged this visit. And I thank you, Mr. President, for your cordial welcome. I greet all of you, the members of this General Assembly. I am grateful for your presence and for your kind attention.

I come before you today with the desire to be able to contribute to that thoughtful meditation on the history and role of this organization, which should accompany and give substance to the anniversary celebrations. The Holy See, in virtue of its specifically spiritual mission, which makes it concerned for the integral good of every human being, has supported the ideals and goals of the United Nations Organization from the very beginning. Although their respective purposes and operative approaches are obviously different, the Church and the United Nations constantly find wide areas of cooperation on the basis of their common concern for the human family. It is this awareness which inspires my thoughts today. They will not dwell on any particular social, political, or economic question; rather, I would like to reflect with you on what the extraordinary changes of the last few years imply, not simply for the present, but for the future of the whole human family.

A Common Human Patrimony

Ladies and gentlemen! On the threshold of a new millennium we are witnessing an extraordinary global acceleration of that quest for freedom which is one of the great dynamics of human history. This phenomenon is not limited to any one part of the world, nor is it the expression of any single culture. Men and women throughout the world, even when threatened by violence, have taken the risk of freedom, asking to be given a place in social, political and economic life which is commensurate with their dignity as free human beings. This universal longing for freedom is truly one of the distinguishing marks of our time.

During my previous visit to the United Nations on October 2, 1979, I noted that the quest for freedom in our time has its basis in those universal rights which human beings enjoy by the very fact of their humanity. It was precisely outrages against human dignity which led the United Nations Organization to formulate, barely three years after its establishment, that *Universal Declaration of Human Rights* which remains one of the highest expressions of the human conscience of our time. In Asia and Africa, in the Americas, in Oceania and Europe, men and women of conviction and courage have appealed to this declaration in support of their claims for a fuller share in the life of society.

There are indeed universal human rights, rooted in the nature of the person, rights which reflect the objective and inviolable demands of a universal moral law.

It is important for us to grasp what might be called the inner structure of this worldwide movement. It is precisely its global character which offers us its first and fundamental "key" and confirms that there are indeed universal human rights, rooted in the nature of the person, rights which reflect the objective and inviolable demands of a universal moral law. These are not abstract points; rather, these rights tell us something important about the actual life of every individual and of every social group. They also remind us that we do not live in an irrational or meaningless world. On the contrary, there is a moral logic which is built into human life and which makes possible dialogue between individuals and peoples. If we want a century of violent coercion to be succeeded by a century of persuasion, we must find a way to discuss the human future intelligibly. The universal moral law written on the human heart is precisely that kind of "grammar" which is needed if the world is to engage this discussion of its future.

In this sense, it is a matter for serious concern that some people today deny the universality of human rights, just as they deny that there is a human nature shared by everyone. To be sure, there is no single model for organizing the politics and economics of human freedom. Different cultures and different historical experiences give rise to different institutional forms of public life in a free and responsible society. But it is one thing to affirm a legitimate pluralism of "forms of freedom," and another to deny any universality or intelligibility to the nature of man or to the human experience. The latter makes the international politics of persuasion extremely difficult, if not impossible.

Taking the Risk of Freedom

The moral dynamics of this universal quest for freedom clearly appeared in Central and Eastern Europe during the nonviolent revolutions of 1989. Unfolding in specific times and places, those historical events nonetheless taught a lesson which goes far beyond a specific geographical location. For the nonviolent revolutions of 1989 demonstrated that the quest for freedom cannot be suppressed. It arises from a recognition of the inestimable dignity and value of the human person, and it cannot fail to be accompanied by a commitment on behalf of the human person. Modern totalitarianism has been, first and foremost, an assault on the dignity of the person, an assault which has gone even to the point of denying the inalienable value of the individual's life. The revolutions of 1989 were made possible by the commitment of brave men and women inspired by a different and ultimately more profound and powerful vision: the vision of man as a creature of intelligence and free will, immersed in a mystery which transcends his own being and endowed with the ability to reflect and the ability to choose—and thus capable of wisdom and virtue. A decisive factor in the success of those nonviolent revolutions was the experience of social solidarity. In the face of regimes backed by the power of propaganda and terror, that solidarity was the moral core of the "power of the powerless," a beacon of hope and an enduring reminder that it is possible for man's historical journey to follow a path which is true to the finest aspirations of the human spirit.

The nonviolent revolutions of 1989 demonstrated that the quest for freedom cannot be suppressed.

Viewing those events from this privileged international forum, one cannot fail to grasp the connection between the values which inspired those peoples' liberation movements and many of the moral commitments inscribed in the *United Nations Charter.* I am thinking for example of the commitment to "reaffirm faith in fundamental human rights (and) in the dignity and worth of the human person," and also the commitment "to promote social progress and better standards of life in larger freedom" (Preamble). The fifty-one states which founded this organization in 1945 truly lit a lamp whose light can scatter the darkness caused by tyranny—a light which can show the way to freedom, peace, and solidarity.

The Rights of Nations

The quest for freedom in the second half of the 20th century has engaged not only individuals but nations as well. Fifty years after the end of the Second World War, it is important to remember that that war was fought because of violations of the rights of nations. Many of those nations suffered grievously for no other reason than that they were deemed "other." Terrible crimes were committed in the name of lethal doctrines which taught the "inferiority" of some nations and cultures. In a certain sense, the United Nations Organization was born from a conviction that such doctrines were antithetical to peace. The charter's commitment to "save future generations from the scourge of war" (Preamble) surely implied a moral commitment to defend every nation and culture from unjust and violent aggression.

Unfortunately, even after the end of the Second World War, the rights of nations continued to be violated. To take but one set of examples, the Baltic States and extensive territories in Ukraine and Belarus were absorbed into the Soviet Union, as had already happened to Armenia, Azerbaijan, and Georgia in the

Caucasus. At the same time the so-called "Peoples' Democracies" of Central and Eastern Europe effectively lost their sovereignty and were required to submit to the will dominating the entire bloc. The result of this artificial division of Europe was the "cold war," a situation of international tension in which the threat of a nuclear holocaust hung over humanity. It was only when freedom was restored to the nations of Central and Eastern Europe that the promise of the peace which should have come with the end of the war began to be realized for many of the victims of that conflict.

The Universal Declaration of Human Rights, *adopted in 1948, spoke eloquently of the rights of persons. But no similar international agreement has yet adequately addressed the rights of nations.*

The *Universal Declaration of Human Rights,* adopted in 1948, spoke eloquently of the rights of persons. But no similar international agreement has yet adequately addressed the rights of nations. This situation must be carefully pondered, for it raises urgent questions about justice and freedom in the world today.

In reality the problem of the full recognition of the rights of peoples and nations has presented itself repeatedly to the conscience of humanity, and has also given rise to considerable ethical and juridical reflection. I am reminded of the debate which took place at the Council of Constance in the 15th century, when the representatives of the Academy of Krakow, headed by Pawel Wodkowic, courageously defended the right of certain European peoples to existence and independence. Still better known is the discussion which went on in that same period at the University of Salamanca with regard to the peoples of the New World. And in our own century, how can I fail to mention the prophetic words of my predecessor, Pope Benedict XV, who in the midst of the First World War reminded everyone that "nations do not die," and invited them "to ponder with serene conscience the rights and the just aspirations of peoples" *(To the Peoples at War and Their Leaders,* July 28, 1915).

Today the problem of nationalities forms part of a new world horizon marked by a great "mobility" which has blurred the ethnic and cultural frontiers of the different peoples, as a result of a variety of processes such as migrations, mass media and the globalization of the economy. And yet, precisely against this horizon of universality we see the powerful re-emergence of a certain ethnic and cultural consciousness, as it were an explosive need for identity and survival, a sort of counterweight to the tendency toward uniformity. This is a phenomenon which must not be underestimated or regarded as a simple leftover of the past. It demands serious interpretation, and a closer examination on the levels of anthropology, ethics and law.

This tension between the particular and the universal can be considered immanent in human beings. By virtue of sharing in the same human nature, people automatically feel that they are members of one great family, as in fact is the case. But as a result of the concrete historical conditioning of this same nature, they are necessarily bound in a more intense way to particular human groups, beginning with the family and going on to the various groups to which they belong and up to the whole of their ethnic and cultural group, which is called, not by accident, a "nation," from the Latin word *nasci* (to be born). This term, enriched with another one, *patria* (fatherland/motherland), evokes the reality of the family. The human condition thus finds itself between these two poles—universality and particularity—with a vital tension between them, an inevitable tension, but singularly fruitful if they are lived in a calm and balanced way.

No one—neither a state nor another nation, nor an international organization—is ever justified in asserting that an individual nation is not worthy of existence.

Upon this anthropological foundation there also rest the "rights of nations," which are nothing but "human rights" fostered at the specific level of community life. A study of these rights is certainly not easy, if we consider the difficulty of defining the very concept of "nation," which cannot be identified *a priori* and necessarily with the state. Such a study must nonetheless be made, if we wish to avoid the errors of the past and ensure a just world order.

A presupposition of a nation's rights is certainly its right to exist. Therefore no one—neither a state nor another nation, nor an international organization—is ever justified in asserting that an individual nation is not worthy of existence. This fundamental right to existence does not necessarily call for sovereignty as a state, since various forms of juridical aggregation between different nations are possible, as occurs for example in federal states, in confederations or in states characterized by broad regional autonomies. There can be historical circumstances in which aggregations different from single state sovereignty can even prove advisable, but only on condition that this takes place in a climate of true freedom, guaranteed by the exercise of the self-determination of the peoples concerned. Its right to exist naturally implies that every nation also enjoys the right to its own language and culture, through which a people expresses and promotes that which I would call its fundamental spiritual "sovereignty." History shows that in extreme circumstances (such as those which occurred in the land where I was born) it is precisely its culture that enables a nation to survive the loss of political and economic independence. Every nation therefore has also the right to shape its life according to its own traditions, excluding, of course, every abuse of basic human rights and in particular the oppression of minorities. Every nation has the right to build its future by providing an appropriate education for the younger generation.

But while the "rights of the nation" express the vital requirements of "particularity," it is no less important to emphasize the requirements of universality, expressed through a clear awareness of the duties which nations have vis-a-vis other nations and humanity as a whole. Foremost among these duties is certainly that of living in a spirit of peace, respect and solidarity with other nations. Thus the exercise of the rights of nations, balanced by the acknowledgment and the practice of duties, promotes a fruitful "exchange of gifts," which strengthens the unity of all mankind.

Respect for Differences

During my pastoral pilgrimages to the communities of the Catholic Church over the past seventeen years, I have been able to enter into dialogue with the rich diversity of nations and cultures in every part of the world. Unhappily, the world has yet to learn how to live with diversity, as recent events in the Balkans and Central Africa have painfully reminded us. The fact of "difference," and the reality of "the other," can sometimes be felt as a burden, or even as a threat. Amplified by historic grievances and exacerbated by the manipulations of the unscrupulous, the fear of "difference" can lead to a denial of the very humanity of "the other," with the result that people fall into a cycle of violence in which no one is spared, not even the children. We are all very familiar today with such situations. At this moment my heart and my prayers turn in a special way to the sufferings of the sorely tried peoples of Bosnia-Herzegovina.

From bitter experience, then, we know that the fear of "difference," especially when it expresses itself in a narrow and exclusive nationalism which denies any rights to "the other," can lead to a true nightmare of violence and terror. And yet if we make the effort to look at matters objectively, we can see that, transcending all the differences which distinguish individuals and peoples, there is a fundamental commonality. For different cultures are but different ways of facing the question of the meaning of personal existence. And it is precisely here that we find one source of the respect which is due to every culture and every nation: every culture is an effort to ponder the mystery of the world and in particular of the human person. It is a way of giving expression to the transcendent dimension of human life. The heart of every culture is its approach to the greatest of all mysteries—the mystery of God.

The heart of every culture is its approach to the greatest of all mysteries— the mystery of God.

Our respect for the culture of others is therefore rooted in our respect for each community's attempt to answer the question of human life. Here we can see how important it is to safeguard the fundamental right to freedom of religion and freedom of conscience, as the cornerstones of the structure of human rights and the foundation of every truly free society. No one is permitted to suppress those rights by using coercive power to impose an answer to the mystery of man.

To cut oneself off from the reality of difference—or, worse, to attempt to stamp out that difference—is to cut oneself off from the possibility of sounding the depths of the mystery of human life. The truth about man is the unchangeable standard by which all cultures are judged, but every culture has something to teach us about one or other dimension of that complex truth. Thus the "difference" which some find so threatening can, through respectful dialogue, become the source of a deeper understanding of the mystery of human existence.

In this context, we need to clarify the essential difference between an unhealthy form of nationalism, which teaches contempt for other nations or cultures, and patriotism, which is a proper love of one's country. True patriotism never seeks to advance the well-being of one's own nation at the expense of others. For in the end this would harm one's own nation as well. Doing wrong damages both aggressor and victim. Nationalism, particularly in its most radical forms, is thus the antithesis of true patriotism. Today we must ensure that extreme nationalism does not continue to give rise to new forms of the aberrations of totalitarianism. This is a commitment which also holds true, obviously, in cases where religion itself is made the basis of nationalism, as unfortunately happens in certain manifestations of so-called "fundamentalism."

Freedom and Moral Truth

Ladies and gentlemen! Freedom is the measure of man's dignity and greatness. Living the freedom sought by individuals and peoples is a great challenge to man's spiritual growth and to the moral vitality of nations. The basic question which we must all face today is the responsible use of freedom, in both its personal and social dimensions. Our reflection must turn then to the question of the moral structure of freedom, which is the inner architecture of the culture of freedom.

Freedom is not simply the absence of tyranny or oppression. Nor is freedom a license to do whatever we like. Freedom has an inner "logic" which distinguishes it and ennobles it: freedom is ordered to the truth, and is fulfilled in man's quest for truth and in man's living in the truth. Detached from the truth about the human person, freedom deteriorates into license in the lives of individuals, and, in political life, it becomes the caprice of the most powerful and the arrogance of power. Far from being a limitation upon freedom or a threat to it, reference to the truth about the human person—a truth universally knowable through the moral law written on the hearts of all—is, in fact, the guarantor of freedom's future.

Freedom is not simply the absence of tyranny or oppression. Nor is freedom a license to do whatever we like.

In the light of what has been said we understand how utilitarianism, the doctrine which defines morality not in terms of what is good but of what is advantageous, threatens the freedom of individuals and nations and obstructs the building of a true culture of freedom. Utilitarianism often has devastating political consequences, because it inspires an aggressive nationalism on the basis of which the subjugation, for example, of a smaller or weaker nation is claimed to be a good thing solely because it corresponds to the national interest. No less grave are the results of economic utilitarianism, which drives more powerful countries to manipulate and exploit weaker ones.

Nationalistic and economic utilitarianism are sometimes combined, a phenomenon which has too often characterized relations between the "North" and the "South." For the emerging countries, the achievement of political independence has too frequently been accompanied by a situation of *de facto* economic dependence on other countries. Indeed, in some cases, the developing world has suffered a regression, such that some countries lack the means of satisfying the essential needs of their people. Such situations offend the conscience of humanity and pose a formidable moral challenge to the human family. Meeting this challenge will obviously require changes in both developing and developed countries. If developing countries are able to offer sure guarantees of the proper management of resources and of assistance received, as well as respect for human rights, by replacing where necessary unjust, corrupt, or authoritarian forms of government with participatory and democratic ones, will they not in this way unleash the best civil and economic energies of their people? And must not the developed countries, for their part, come to renounce strictly utilitarian approaches and develop new approaches inspired by greater justice and solidarity?

Yes, distinguished ladies and gentlemen! The international economic scene needs an ethic of solidarity, if participation, economic growth and a just distribution of goods are to characterize the future of humanity. The international cooperation called for by the charter of the United Nations for "solving international problems of an economic, social, cultural, or humanitarian character" (art. 1.3) cannot be conceived exclusively in terms of help and assistance, or even by considering the eventual returns on the resources provided. When millions of people are suffering from a poverty which means hunger, malnutrition, sickness, illiteracy and degradation, we must not only remind ourselves that no one has a right to exploit another for his own advantage. Also and above all we must recommit ourselves to that solidarity which enables others to live out, in the actual circumstances of their economic and political lives, the creativity which is a distinguishing mark of the human person and the true source of the wealth of nations in today's world.

The United Nations
and the Future of Freedom

As we face these enormous challenges, how can we fail to acknowledge the role of the United Nations Organization? Fifty years after its founding, the need for such an organization is even more obvious. But we also have a better understanding, on the basis of experience, that the effectiveness of this great instrument for harmonizing and coordinating international life depends on the international culture and ethic which it supports and expresses. The United Nations Organization needs to rise more and more above the cold status of an administrative institution and to become a moral center where all the nations of the world feel at home and develop a shared awareness of being, as it were, a "family of nations." The idea of "family" immediately evokes something more than simple functional relations or a mere convergence of interests. The family is by nature a community based on mutual trust, mutual support and sincere respect. In an authentic family the strong do not dominate; instead, the weaker members, because of their very weakness, are all the more welcomed and served.

Raised to the level of the "family of nations," these sentiments ought to be, even before law itself, the very fabric of relations between peoples. The United Nations has the historic, even momentous, task of promoting this qualitative leap in international life, not only by serving as a center of effective mediation for the resolution of conflicts but also by fostering values, attitudes and concrete initiatives of solidarity which prove capable of raising the level of relations between nations from the "organizational" to a more "organic" level, from simple "existence with" others to "existence for" others, in a fruitful exchange of gifts, primarily for the good of the weaker nations but even so, a clear harbinger of greater good for everyone.

Now is the time for new hope, which calls us to expel the paralyzing burden of cynicism from the future of politics and of human life.

Only on this condition shall we attain an end not only to "wars of combat" but also to "cold wars." It will ensure not only the legal equality of all peoples but also their active participation in the building of a better future, and not only respect for individual cultural identities, but full esteem for them as a common treasure belonging to the cultural patrimony of mankind. Is this not the ideal held up by the charter of the United Nations when it sets as the basis of the organization "the principle of the sovereign equality of all its members" (art. 2.1), or when it commits it to "develop friendly relations between nations based on respect for the principle of equal rights and of self-determination" (art. 1.2)? This is the high road which must be followed to the end, even if this involves, when necessary, appropriate modifications in the operating model of the United Nations, so as to take into account everything that has happened in this half century, with so many new peoples experiencing freedom and legitimately aspiring to "be" and to "count for" more.

None of this should appear as an unattainable utopia. Now is the time for new hope, which calls us to expel the paralyzing burden of cynicism from the future of politics and of human life. The anniversary which we are celebrating invites us to do this by reminding us of the idea of "united nations," an idea which bespeaks mutual trust, security and solidarity. Inspired by the example of all those who have taken the risk of freedom, can we not recommit ourselves also to taking the risk of solidarity—and thus the risk of peace?

Beyond Fear: The Civilization of Love

It is one of the great paradoxes of our time that man, who began the period we call "modernity" with a self-confident assertion of his "coming of age" and "autonomy," approaches the end of the 20th century fearful of himself, fearful of what he might be capable of, fearful for the future. Indeed, the second half of the 20th century has seen the unprecedented phenomenon of a humanity uncertain about the very likelihood of a future, given the threat of nuclear war. That danger, mercifully, appears to have receded—and everything that might make it return needs to be rejected firmly and universally. All the same, fear for the future and of the future remains.

In order to ensure that the new millennium now approaching will witness a new flourishing of the human spirit, mediated through an authentic culture of freedom, men and women must learn to conquer fear. We must learn not to be afraid, we must rediscover a spirit of hope and a spirit of trust. Hope is not empty optimism springing from a naive confidence that the future will necessarily be better than the past. Hope and trust are the premise of responsible activity and are nurtured in that inner sanctuary of conscience where "man is alone with God" (*Gaudium et Spes*, n. 16) and thus perceives that he is not alone amid the enigmas of existence, for he is surrounded by the love of the Creator!

We must learn not to be afraid, we must rediscover a spirit of hope and a spirit of trust.

Hope and trust: these may seem matters beyond the purview of the United Nations. But they are not. The politics of nations, with which your organization is principally concerned, can never ignore the transcendent, spiritual dimension of the human experience, and could never ignore it without harming the cause of man and the cause of human freedom. Whatever diminishes man—whatever shortens the horizon of man's aspiration to goodness—harms the cause of freedom. In order to recover our hope and our trust at the end of this century of sorrows, we must regain sight of that transcendent horizon of possibility to which the soul of man aspires.

As a Christian, my hope and trust are centered on Jesus Christ, the 2,000th anniversary of whose birth will be celebrated at the coming of the new millennium. We Christians believe that his death and resurrection fully revealed God's love and his care for all creation. Jesus Christ is for us God made man, and made a part of the history of humanity. Precisely for this reason, Christian hope for the world and its future extends to every human person. Because of the radiant humanity of Christ, nothing genuinely human fails to touch the hearts of Christians. Faith in Christ does not impel us to intolerance. On the contrary, it obliges us to engage others in a respectful dialogue. Love of Christ does not distract us from interest in others, but rather invites us to responsibility for them, to the exclusion of no one and indeed, if anything, with a special concern for the weakest and the suffering. Thus, as we approach the 2,000th anniversary of the birth of Christ, the Church asks only to be able to propose respectfully this message of salvation, and to be able to promote, in charity and service, the solidarity of the entire human family.

Ladies and gentlemen! I come before you, as did my predecessor Pope Paul VI exactly thirty years ago, not as one who exercises temporal power—these are his words—nor as a religious leader seeking special privileges for his community. I come before you as a witness: a witness to human dignity, a witness to hope, a witness to the conviction that the destiny of all nations lies in the hands of a merciful providence.

We must overcome our fear of the future. But we will not be able to overcome it completely unless we do so together. The "answer" to that fear is neither coercion nor repression, nor the imposition of one social "model" on the entire world. The answer to the fear which darkens human existence at the end of the 20th century is the common effort to build the civilization of love, founded on the universal values of peace, solidarity, justice and liberty. And the "soul" of the civilization of love is the culture of freedom: the freedom of individuals and the freedom of nations, lived in self-giving solidarity and responsibility.

We must not be afraid of the future. We must not be afraid of man. It is no accident that we are here. Each and every human person has been created in the "image and likeness" of the one who is the origin of all that is. We have within us the capacities for wisdom and virtue. With these gifts, and with the help of God's grace, we can build in the next century and the next millennium a civilization worthy of the human person, a true culture of freedom. We can and must do so! And in doing so, we shall see that the tears of this century have prepared the ground for a new springtime of the human spirit.

Giants' Stadium

Homily at a Mass in Giants' Stadium, East Rutherford, New Jersey, October 5, 1995

"Thy kingdom come!" (Mt 6:10).

Dear Archbishop McCarrick and my other brother bishops, dear brothers and sisters in Christ,

Each day in the "Our Father" we pray, "Thy kingdom come!" (cf. Mt 6:9-13). In today's Gospel we have heard about Jesus sending out his disciples to proclaim that "the kingdom of God is at hand" (cf. Lk 10:9).

Today we are celebrating the good news of God's kingdom here in Giants' Stadium, in the Archdiocese of Newark, in New Jersey—the Garden State. I greet the whole Catholic community of Newark, and in a special way your pastor and my faithful friend, Archbishop McCarrick, whom I thank for his warm words of welcome. I greet God's beloved people from all of New Jersey—the bishops, priests, deacons, seminarians, women and men religious, parents, children, the young, the old, the sick. These greetings include our brothers and sisters of Eastern-rite dioceses, whose presence gives vibrant witness to the rich diversity of God's holy Church. I am also grateful to the civic leaders of city and state and the representatives of the various religious denominations who have wished to share this moment of prayer with us.

[Spoken in Spanish]: I wish to greet all Spanish-speaking people present at this Mass, for the Church in the United States also speaks Spanish. I wish to encourage you to let your faith be ever more visible in your daily lives, in the care of your families, in your professional and social commitments. Never lose the joy and generosity with which you have learned to follow our Lord Jesus Christ!

What is this kingdom which Jesus announced and which the Church continues to proclaim down the centuries? First, it is the affirmation of God's dominion over all creation. As Creator, he reigns over the world he has made. But the kingdom means more. It means that God is present as Lord in this world. The kingdom is present above all in Jesus Christ, the eternal Son, who became flesh and dwelt among us (cf. Jn 1:14). Furthermore, the kingdom embraces us all. By his death on the cross and his resurrection from the dead, Christ redeemed us from our sins and gave us new life in the Spirit. Through the paschal mystery—as St. Paul writes—God "has rescued us from the power of darkness and brought us into the kingdom of his beloved Son" (Col 1:13).

Like the people of Israel spoken of in the first reading, who gathered around the priest Ezra and listened to the word of God with profound emotion (cf. Neh 8:5), we have stood to hear the message of God's presence and love which the liturgy presents to us this evening.

Nehemiah is speaking of the time after the Babylonian captivity, when the Jewish people returned to their homeland. At the end of the reading, "Ezra blessed the Lord, the great God, and all the people, their hands raised high, answered: 'Amen, Amen'" (Neh 8:6). This great "Amen" is echoed at every Mass when, at the end of the Eucharistic prayer, we offer glory and honor to the Father through the Son, in the Holy Spirit. With this "Amen" the whole community acknowledges the real presence on the altar of Jesus Christ, the living and eternal Word of the Father. In the spirit of this great "Amen," all of us gathered here in Giants Stadium praise Jesus Christ for the newness of life (cf. Rom 6:4) which he gives us in the Holy Spirit! Praised be our Lord and Savior Jesus Christ!

The Gospel shows us Jesus sending his disciples to proclaim the good news of the kingdom of God (cf. Lk 10:1). He tells them openly that some people will ignore or reject their message. But such human resistance will not prevent the coming of the kingdom (cf. Lk 10:10-11). The kingdom is always present because the Father himself has brought it into the world through the passion, death and resurrection of his Son Jesus Christ. From the day of Pentecost, the Holy Spirit never ceases to communicate the power of Christ's kingship, and to invite men and women to find salvation in the one who is "the way, and the truth, and the life" (cf. Jn 14:6).

In order to bring us this salvation, Jesus established the Church to be "a kind of sacrament—a sign and instrument—of intimate union with God and of the unity of all mankind" *(Lumen Gentium,* n. 1). Among the many magnificent images which the Bible uses to describe the Church, one of the most beautiful is that of the house in which God dwells with his people (cf. Eph 2:19-22; 1 Tim

3:15). The Lord wants his Church to "make a home" in the midst of every people, grafting the gifts of salvation onto the history and culture of each nation. In today's Gospel, Jesus sends his disciples into people's houses, to bring them his peace (cf. Lk 10:5). In every place where people make their homes and live their lives, a disciple of Jesus must arrive to say: "The kingdom of God is at hand" (cf. Lk 10:9).

We give thanks to God for the way in which the Church has "made a home" in America.

Tonight we give thanks to God for the way in which the Church has "made a home" in America. From the beginning, in this new land the Church grew out of the faith of peoples from many cultural and ethnic backgrounds, embracing the indigenous people and settlers alike. Everywhere we see the results of the labors of countless priests, religious sisters and brothers, Christian families and individual lay men and women who made the Church present in American society through a great network of parishes, schools, hospitals and charitable institutions. This proud heritage should serve as an inspiration and an incentive for you as you seek to meet the challenges of our own times.

The Church must continue to build God's spiritual house in America! Here in the Church in Newark, last year's archdiocesan synod put the whole Catholic community in a state of mission. In particular, the synod appealed to the laity to work for God's kingdom by their efforts to shape society in accordance with God's designs. No aspect of life—whether in the family, in the workplace, in schools, in economic, political or social activities—can be withdrawn from God's dominion (cf. *Lumen Gentium,* n. 36). As we prepare to celebrate the 2,000th anniversary of Christ's birth, your synod, like the whole Church, recognized the need for a new evangelization, a new and vital proclamation of the Gospel aimed at integrating your faith ever more fully into the fabric of your daily lives. In the words of the Second Vatican Council, wherever there is little concern for seeking what is true and good, and wherever conscience is blinded by being accustomed to sin (cf. *Gaudium et Spes,* n. 16), there the Church must make a supreme effort to teach the objective truths of the moral order, form consciences, call people to conversion and make present the inexhaustible riches of God's mercy in the sacraments, and especially in the sacrament of penance.

The Christian life is a dynamic reality: the seed of faith sown in our hearts through baptism must ripen and mature into a rich harvest of union with God and good works in the service of others. Jesus uses the image of the harvest to describe the Church's role in the world. From generation to generation, in every time and place, the seed sown by God in human history through the death and resurrection of Christ continues to mature and awaits the harvest.

Jesus reminds us that more workers for the harvest are urgently needed, and he commands us to pray for them: "The harvest is rich but the workers are few; therefore ask the harvest-master to send workers to his harvest" (Lk 10:2). The question of vocations is vital to the

Church. Everyone has a vocation: parents, teachers, students, workers, professional people, people who are retired. Everyone has something to do for God. We must pray that young people especially will listen to the Lord's call to serve as priests, as religious sisters and brothers, as missionaries at home and in other lands. Young people of Newark and New Jersey, young Americans, the Lord needs you! The Church needs you!

We must pray that young people especially will listen to the Lord's call to serve as priests, as religious sisters and brothers, as missionaries at home and in other lands.

Compared to many other parts of the world, the United States is a privileged land. Yet, even here there is much poverty and human suffering. There is much need for love and the works of love; there is need for social solidarity. Early Americans were proud of their strong sense of individual responsibility, but that did not lead them to build a radically "individualistic" society. They built a community-based society, with a great openness and sensitivity to the needs of their neighbors.

Quite close to the shores of New Jersey there rises a universally known landmark which stands as an enduring witness to the American tradition of welcoming the stranger, and which tells us something important about the kind of nation America has aspired to be. It is the Statue of Liberty, with its celebrated poem: "Give me your tired, your poor, your huddled masses yearning to breathe free.... Send these, the homeless, tempest-tossed to me." Is present-day America becoming less sensitive, less caring toward the poor, the weak, the stranger, the needy? It must not! Today, as before, the United States is called to be a hospitable society, a welcoming culture. If America were to turn in on itself, would this not be the beginning of the end of what constitutes the very essence of the "American experience"?

To a great extent, the story of America has been the story of long and difficult struggles to overcome the prejudices which excluded certain categories of people from a full share in the country's life: first, the struggle against religious intolerance, then the struggle against racial discrimination and in favor of civil rights for everyone. Sadly, today a new class of people is being excluded. When the unborn child—the "stranger in the womb"—is declared to be beyond the protection of society, not only are America's deepest traditions radically undermined and endangered, but a moral blight is brought upon society. I am also thinking of threats to the elderly, the severely handicapped and all those who do not seem to have any social usefulness. When innocent human beings are declared inconvenient or burdensome, and thus unworthy of legal and social protection, grievous damage is done to the moral foundations of the democratic community. The right to life is the first of all rights. It is the foundation of democratic liberties and the keystone of the edifice of civil society. Both as Americans and as followers of Christ, American Catholics must be committed to the defense of life in all its stages and in every condition.

Dear sisters and brothers, Christ pointed the Church and the whole human family toward the future when he rolled away the stone from the entrance to the tomb and unveiled the mystery of new life. In his resurrection, the Lord revealed the new creation, the promise of new heavens and a new earth (cf. 2 Pet 3:13). As Christians, we live by faith and in hope. We wait for the return of the Lord as the judge of the living and the dead. We await his return in glory, the coming of God's kingdom in its fullness. That is the constant invitation of the psalms: "Wait for the Lord with courage; be stouthearted, and wait for the Lord" (Ps 27:14).

When the unborn child—the "stranger in the womb"—is declared to be beyond the protection of society, not only are America's deepest traditions radically undermined and endangered, but a moral blight is brought upon society.

Our confidence in the future which God has opened before us enables us to see this earthly life in its proper light. In the perspective of God's kingdom we discern the true value of all the accomplishments of human civilization and culture, of all our achievements, our struggles and our sufferings. As Americans, you are rightly proud of your country's great achievements. As Christians, you know that all things human are the soil in which the kingdom of God is meant to take root and mature! To the Church in the United States, to you, the Church in Newark, I make this appeal: Do not make an idol of any temporal reality! "Know that the kingdom of God is at hand" (cf. Lk 10:11). "Wait for the Lord with courage; be stouthearted" (Ps 27:14). Hope in the Lord! Amen.

Aqueduct Racetrack

Homily at a Mass in Aqueduct Racetrack, Queens, New York, October 6, 1995

Dear brothers and sisters in Christ,

Jesus' words in today's Gospel bring me back to my youth and remind me of a song we used to sing in my home parish at Wadowice. The words of that song are very simple, but at the same time very profound:

"Come, Holy Spirit, we stand in need of your grace. Make us grow in the heavenly knowledge you have revealed. Make it easy for us to understand it, and by our perseverance may it remain in us. Enlightened by that truth, we shall be confirmed in goodness."

These words express well the theology of the Holy Spirit, through whom the Father reveals what is "hidden from the learned and the clever" (Mt 11:25), and through whom the Son reveals the Father (cf. Mt 11:27). The Spirit, in fact, is the active agent of the Church's evangelizing mission. For this reason, the Church constantly invokes the Holy Spirit upon individual communities, and today we renew that invocation here, at the Aqueduct Racetrack in Queens.

I am happy to see such a representative gathering of the faithful of this local Church. I greet all of you with warm affection: Your stalwart pastor, Bishop Thomas Daily, my other brother bishops, the priests, deacons, religious and laity from the Diocese of Brooklyn and many other dioceses. At the same time my greetings go to the leaders of the various religious denominations and the civil authorities from both local and state government. I am pleased also to greet the different councils of the Knights of Columbus from the United States and Canada which are represented here, together with the supreme knight, Mr. Virgil Dechant. Gathered around the altar of the Lord, let us offer this sacred act of worship, asking for strength to meet the challenges of the new evangelization to which the Holy Spirit is calling the Church of God.

[Spoken in Spanish]: I know that there are many Spanish-speaking people, families and communities present at this Mass. In the heart of the Pope, you have a special place. To each one I express my sincere love and affection in the Lord.

The theme of this morning's holy Mass is the "progress of peoples." This is an appropriate issue in the context of my visit to the United States for the 50th anniversary of the United Nations organization. The Pope's presence at that international forum is in fact an act of evangelization, aimed at serving the progress of humanity in the great family of nations which that world organization represents.

The "progress of peoples" is closely connected with the proclamation of Christ's message of salvation and hope. Of this salvation Isaiah speaks in the first reading:

"The people who walked in darkness have seen a great light. Upon those who dwelt in the land of gloom a light has shone" (Is 9:1). This darkness stands for the spiritual darkness which sometimes envelops people, nations and history itself in its desolate mantle. Certainly the 20th century has witnessed such periods of gloom. The two world wars were times of great darkness which plunged peoples and nations into immense suffering. For many people, the 20th century continues to be a time of terrible anguish and torture. From the depths of such sad experiences the human family searches for a path of justice and peace.

[Spoken in Spanish]: Isaiah goes on to suggest that genuine justice and peace, the authentic progress of peoples, is centered on God's plan to send a Savior. For he writes: "A child is born to us, a son is given us.... His dominion is vast and forever peaceful.... He confirms and sustains by judgment and justice, both now and forever" (Is 9:5-6). Here the prophet is speaking of the Messiah whose arrival Israel so eagerly awaited. This is the Messiah so anxiously looked to by modern men and women, especially when they have been immersed in the devastating experiences of war, of concentration camps, of brutality and contempt for human dignity.

It is here that the words of Jesus, who is our salvation and our hope, take on a special meaning: "Come to me, all you who are weary and find life burdensome, and I will refresh you" (Mt 11:28). Christ himself carried a burden, and his burden—the cross—was made heavier by the sins of us all. But Christ did not avoid the cross; he accepted it and carried it willingly. Moreover, he now stands beside those weighed down by trials and persecutions, remaining beside them to the end. It is for all people and with all people that he carries the cross to

Calvary, and it is there that for all of us he is nailed to his cross. He dies the death of a criminal, the most humiliating death known to the world at that time. That is why to those in our own century who carry terrible burdens he is able to say: "Come to me! I am your brother in suffering. There is no humiliation or bitterness which I do not know!"

It is precisely through the Gospel of the cross and through his resurrection that Christ lays the foundations for the advancement of God's kingdom in the world. The presence of this kingdom opens to us the dimension of eternity in God, and discloses the deepest meaning of our efforts to improve life here on earth. People everywhere thirst for a full and free life worthy of the human person. There is a great desire for political, social and economic institutions which will help individuals and nations to affirm and develop their dignity (cf. *Gaudium et Spes*, n. 9).

It is precisely through the Gospel of the cross and through his resurrection that Christ lays the foundations for the advancement of God's kingdom in the world.

What kind of society is worthy of the human person? The Church responds with the unique perspective of salvation history. She proclaims the truth that the word of God, through whom all things were made, was himself made flesh and dwelt among us. He entered the world's history—our history—as a man; he took on our history and made it complete. By his resurrection he became Lord and was given full power in heaven and on earth. Thus through the power of his Spirit, Christ is now at work in our hearts and in our world. The Spirit instills in us a desire for the world to come, but he also inspires, purifies and strengthens those noble longings by which we strive to make earthly life more human (cf. *Gaudium et Spes*, n. 38).

In the midst of the magnificent scientific and technological civilization of which America is proud...is there room for the mystery of God?

Dear friends, we are gathered together in this enormous metropolis of New York, considered by many to be the zenith of modern civilization and progress, a symbol of America and American life. For more than 200 years people of different nations, languages and cultures have come here, bringing memories and traditions of the "old country," while at the same time becoming part of a new nation. America has a reputation the world over, a reputation of power, prestige and wealth. But not everyone here is powerful; not everyone here is rich. In fact, America's sometimes extravagant affluence often conceals much hardship and poverty.

From the viewpoint of the kingdom of God we must therefore ask a very basic question: have the people living in this huge metropolis lost sight of the blessings which belong to the poor in spirit? In the midst of the magnificent scientific and technological civilization of which America is proud, and especially here in Queens, in Brooklyn, in New York, is there room for the mystery of God? That mystery which is "revealed to the merest children" (Mt 11:25), the mystery of the Father and the Son in the unity of the Holy Spirit, the mystery of divine love which is the source of everything? Is there room for the revelation of life—that transcendent life which Christ brings us at the price of his cross and through the victory of his resurrection?

The Gospel of the kingdom of God is open to every aspect of earthly progress which helps people to discover and enter the space of divine life, the space of eternal salvation. This is the work of the Church; this is the work which the Holy Spirit will accomplish through all of us, if only we will heed the truth he reveals and be confirmed in goodness!

In practical terms, this truth tells us that there can be no life worthy of the human person without a culture—and a legal system—that honors and defends marriage and the family. The well-being of individuals and communities depends on the healthy state of the family. A few years ago, your National Commission on America's Urban Families concluded, and I quote: "The family trend of our time is the de-institutionalization of marriage and the steady disintegration of the mother-father child-raising unit.... No domestic trend is more threatening to the well-being of our children and to our long-term national security" *(Report,* January 1993). I quote these words to show that it is not just the Pope and the Church who speak with concern about these important issues.

Society must strongly reaffirm the right of the child to grow up in a family in which, as far as possible, both parents are present. Fathers of families must accept their full share of responsibility for the lives and upbringing of their children. Both parents must spend time with their children, and be personally interested in their moral and religious education. Children need not only material support from their parents, but more importantly a secure, affectionate and morally correct family environment.

There can be no life worthy of the human person without a culture—and a legal system—that honors and defends marriage and the family.

Catholic parents must learn to form their family as a "domestic church," a church in the home as it were, where God is honored, his law is respected, prayer is a normal event, virtue is transmitted by word and example, and everyone shares the hopes, the problems and sufferings of everyone else. All this is not to advocate a return to some outdated style of living. It is to return to the roots of human development and human happiness!

The truth which Christ reveals tells us that we must support one another and work together with others, despite cultural, social or religious differences. It challenges us to be involved. It gives us the courage to see Christ in our neighbor and to serve him there. And, in imitation of our divine Master who said, "Come to me, all you who are weary and find life burdensome" (Mt 11:28), we ought to invite others to come to us by stretching out a helping hand to those in need, by welcoming the newcomer, by speaking words of comfort to the afflicted. This is the goodness in which the Holy Spirit confirms us! This is how you—women and men, young people and old, married couples and singles, parents, children and families, students and teachers, professional people, those who work and those who are suffering the terrible burden of unemployment—this is how everyone can make a positive contribution to America and help to transform your culture into a vibrant culture of life.

This, dear brothers and sisters, is what it means to work for the kingdom of God in America today. This is the way which leads to the true progress of nations and peoples; it is the path of justice and peace, the light which shines in the darkness, the yoke which is easy and the burden which is light. This is where our souls will find rest.

"Come, Holy Spirit, we stand in need of your grace. Make us grow in the heavenly knowledge you have revealed. Make it easy for us to understand it, and by our perseverance may it remain in us. Enlightened by that truth, we will be confirmed in goodness." Amen.

St. Joseph's Seminary

Address to the seminarians during evening prayer at St. Joseph's Seminary in Yonkers, New York, October 6, 1995

"O wisdom, O holy word of God, you govern all creation with your strong yet tender care. Come, teach us the way of wisdom." (Advent antiphon, December 17).

Dear brothers and sisters in Christ,

These words of the Advent antiphon come to mind as we listen to the reading of today's vespers here in this beautiful chapel of St. Joseph's Seminary in Dunwoodie. In his First Letter to the Corinthians, St. Paul writes of wisdom: "What we utter is God's wisdom: a mysterious, a hidden wisdom. God planned it before all ages for our glory" (1 Cor 2:7). But what wisdom is this? St. Paul is speaking of God's plan for our salvation, the plan brought to completion by the eternal Word, divine wisdom himself, the Son who is of one being with the Father, the holy Word of God spoken of in the Advent

56

antiphon. This is the Word, of course, of whom St. John speaks in the prologue of his Gospel: "In the beginning was the Word. The Word was in God's presence and the Word was God.... The Word became flesh and made his dwelling among us, and we have seen his glory" (Jn 1:1,14).

The wisdom of the cross is at the heart of the life and ministry of every priest.

Dear members of this seminary community, and you from other seminaries, as well as the many people outside this chapel who have joined us: Eternal wisdom became flesh, being born of the Virgin Mary. This is why we pray to Mary as the "seat of wisdom," *sedes sapientiae.* Wisdom, the person of the Son, was conceived in Mary's womb by the power of the Holy Spirit. Born of her flesh, Jesus is eternal wisdom, the Son of God, whose glory is revealed in his passing from the cross to the resurrection. It is crucial that you seminarians understand this because, as St. Paul says, the "rulers of this age" did not understand God's wisdom at the time, for—he writes— "if they had known it, they would never have crucified the Lord of glory" (1 Cor 2:8). And many do not understand it today.

Even some who call themselves Christians do not recognize that Christ is the eternal Son of the Father who brings true wisdom into the world. For this reason, they do not understand or accept the teachings of the Church. Perhaps you have already been confronted by this. You will certainly have to confront it as priests. If you are to become priests, it will be for the purpose—above all other purposes—of proclaiming the word of God and feeding God's people with the body and blood of Christ. If you do this faithfully, teaching the wisdom that comes from above, you will often be ignored as Christ was ignored, and even rejected as Christ was rejected. "I preach Christ and Christ crucified," says St. Paul (cf. 1 Cor 1:23).

Why has the Pope come to Dunwoodie to give you such a serious message? Because in Christ we are friends (cf. Jn 15:15), and friends can talk about serious matters. If there is one challenge facing the Church and her priests today, it is the challenge of transmitting the Christian message whole and entire, without letting it be emptied of its substance. The Gospel cannot be reduced to mere human wisdom. Salvation lies not in clever human words or schemes, but in the cross and resurrection of our Lord Jesus Christ. The wisdom of the cross is at the heart of the life and ministry of every priest. This is the sublime "science" which, above all other learning, the seminary is meant to impart to you: "The Spirit we have received is not the world's spirit but God's Spirit.... We speak...not in words of human wisdom, but in words taught by the Spirit" (1 Cor 2:12-13).

This is also the framework of the service I have tried to render at the United Nations during these days. If the Pope did something other than what St. Paul calls "interpreting spiritual things in spiritual terms" (1 Cor 2:13), what message could he preach? How could I justify my presence and my speaking to that assembly? My task is not to speak in purely human terms about merely human values, but in spiritual terms about spiritual values, which are ultimately what make us fully human.

Over the magnificent doors of this chapel I am able to read words that have a very special meaning for me: *Aperite portas Redemptori.* These were my words to the peoples of the world at the very beginning of my pontificate: "Help the Pope," I said, "and all those who wish to serve Christ and with Christ's power to serve the human person and the whole of mankind. Do not be afraid! Open wide the doors for Christ!" (Homily, St. Peter's Square, October 22, 1978).

Do not be afraid, I say, because great courage is required if we are to open the doors to Christ, if we are to let Christ enter into our hearts so fully that we can say with St. Paul, "The life I live now is not my own; Christ is living in me" (Gal 2:20). Conquering fear is the first and indispensable step for the priest if he is to open the doors, first of his own heart, then of the hearts of the people he serves, to Christ the Redeemer. You need courage to follow Christ, especially when you recognize that so much of our dominant culture is a culture of flight from God, a culture which displays a not-so-hidden contempt for human life, beginning with the lives of the unborn, and extending to contempt for the frail and the elderly. Some people say that the Pope speaks too much about the "culture of death." But these are times in which—as I wrote in my encyclical *Evangelium Vitae*— "choices once unanimously considered criminal and rejected by the common moral sense are gradually becoming socially acceptable" (n. 4). The Church cannot ignore what is happening.

And yet, this is only one part of the picture. The complete picture is what I wrote at the beginning of the same encyclical: "The Gospel of Life is at the heart of Jesus' message. Lovingly received day after day by the Church, it is to be preached with dauntless fidelity as 'good news' to the people of every age and culture" (n. 1). Therefore, dear seminarians, you must not be afraid to confront the "wisdom of this world" with the certainty of the teachings of Christ in which you are grounded, but above all with the love of Christ, with the compassion and the mercy of Christ, who—like the Father—desires everyone to be saved and to come to the knowledge of the truth (cf. 1 Tim 2:4). The disciple cannot be greater than the master (cf. Mt 10:24). You will not become priests to be served, or to lord it over others, but to serve others (cf. Mt 20:28), especially the poorest of the poor, the materially poor and the spiritually poor.

You need courage to follow Christ, especially when you recognize that so much of our dominant culture is a culture of flight from God.

Open the doors of your hearts in order that Christ may enter and bring you his joy. The Church needs joyful priests, capable of bringing true joy to God's people, which is the good news in all its truth and transforming power.

This evening's reading from St. Paul is very appropriate for the seminary community. Why are you here as seminarians? Why are you here, members of the faculty and others who help to prepare seminarians for the priesthood? Is it not to "know the mind of the Lord"? The seminarian must ask himself: Is Christ calling me?

Does he wish me to be his priest? If you answer "yes," then the great work of the seminary is to help you to put off "the natural man," to leave behind "the old man," that is, the unspiritual man who used to be, in order to experience the action of the Holy Spirit and to understand the things of the spirit of God. You must enter into an intimate relationship with the Holy Spirit and with all his gifts, in order that the Lord's intentions for you may become clear. This is another way of expressing the need for wisdom. Indeed, the seminary must be a school of wisdom. Here you must live with your patron, St. Joseph, and with Mary, the mother of Jesus; and in the silence of this intimacy you will learn that wisdom of which St. Luke speaks: "Jesus for his part progressed steadily in wisdom and age and grace before God and men" (Lk 2:52).

I have to say a word of appreciation to the rector and his associates for recently incorporating into the seminary program a full year devoted exclusively to spiritual formation. This will be a precious time for advancing in wisdom and holiness, that wisdom and holiness which are essential for the priesthood.

Next year, St. Joseph's Seminary will celebrate its 100th anniversary. It is providential that the same year, 1996, will be a year of evangelization in the Church in New York. It helps us remember the countless souls, redeemed by the blood of Christ, who have been helped toward salvation by the thousands of priests trained in this seminary. You will join them in continuing the work of salvation, which will never end until, as Jesus prayᵉ all will become one in him as he is one with the ᵣ (cf. Jn 17:21-23).

I thank Cardinal O'Connor, your O'Brien, the faculty and staff and all w.

tee here for this special privilege of praying with you. Above all, I encourage you, the seminarians, to be unselfish in answering the call of Christ and in offering your lives to his Church. Do not be afraid! If you begin to lose courage, turn to Mary, seat of wisdom; with her at your side, you will never be afraid. Amen.

Central Park

Homily at a Mass in Central Park, New York City, October 7, 1995

"Come Holy Spirit..."!

Dear friends in Christ,

Today's liturgy is full of references to the Holy Spirit. Even as we pray for the Spirit to come among us, he is already here. He is here in so many of you. He is here above all in the action of the Mass, the most sacred rite of our faith. You are here, I trust, not out of simple curiosity to see the Pope, but because of the Mass, because the Holy Spirit is leading us all to Christ!

For me it is a great joy to look out at so many wonderful people, and to greet Cardinal O'Connor and all the bishops from the New York metropolitan province and elsewhere, as well as all the priests, religious and laity of the archdiocese, and the civil authorities of ᵗʰ state and city of New York. My warm and affecᵗ· greetings go to the sick and the handicapped

It is especially wonderful to see so many young people. I can hardly believe we are not back in Denver, which was such an enriching experience. So many thousands of young people astonished everyone with their spirit and their faith. I remember clearly that many people wondered and worried that the young people of America would not come to the World Youth Day, or, if they did come, that they would be a problem. Instead, the young people's joy, their hunger for the truth, their desire to be united all together in the body of Christ, made clear to everyone that many, very many young people of America have values and ideals which seldom make the headlines. Is it any wonder that the Pope loves you!

[Spoken in Spanish]: The Pope also loves the sons and daughters of the Church who speak Spanish! Many of you have been born here or have lived here for a long time. Others are more recent arrivals. But you all bear the mark of your cultural heritage, deeply rooted in the Catholic tradition. Keep alive that faith and culture!

I know this is not Denver, this is New York! The great New York! This is Central Park. The beautiful surroundings of Central Park invite us to reflect on a more sublime beauty: the beauty of every human being, made in the image and likeness of God (cf. Gen 1:26), and the beauty that is God living in our hearts through the Holy Spirit. At Denver we meditated on this new life: "I came that they may have life, and have it abundantly" (Jn 10:10). In Manila, last January, millions of young people gathered to meditate on how that new life in the Holy Spirit makes us apostles of Christ's kingdom: "As the Father has sent me, so am I sending you" (Jn 20:21). Now, today, here in Central Park we are continuing the same spiritual pilgrimage, getting ready for the next World Youth Day, in Paris in 1997. I am very grateful for all that is being done in parishes and dioceses all over the world to bring young people into the spirit of this great spiritual pilgrimage across the world, which started in Rome in 1984, then brought us to Buenos Aires in Argentina, to Santiago de Compostela in Spain, to Jasna Gora and Czestochowa in Poland, to Denver, to Manila, and next to Paris. At the ecumenical level, a similar spiritual pilgrimage is made at Taize in France. The driving force of all this movement of young people is always the Holy Spirit.

In our bodies we are a mere speck in the vast created universe, but by virtue of our souls we transcend the whole material world.

The Spirit of God who, we are told in the Book of Genesis, breathed upon the waters at the very beginning of creation (cf. 1:2), is the same Spirit of life who was breathed into man, so that "man became a living being" (2:7). This is what makes us different from every other creature. In our bodies we are a mere speck in the vast created universe, but by virtue of our souls we transcend the whole material world. I invite you to reflect on what makes each one of you truly marvelous and unique. Only a human being like you can think and speak and share your thoughts in different languages with other human beings all over the world, and through the guage express the beauty of art and poetry and

and literature and the theater, and so many other uniquely human accomplishments.

And most important of all, only God's precious human beings are capable of loving. Love makes us seek what is good; love makes us better persons. It is love that prompts men and women to marry and form a family, to have children. It is love that prompts others to embrace the religious life or become priests. Love makes you reach out to others in need, whoever they are, wherever they are. Every genuine human love is a reflection of the love that is God himself, to the point where the First Letter of St. John says: "The man without love has known nothing of God; for God is love" (4:8).

Today is the feast of the Holy Rosary of the Blessed Virgin Mary. The readings of the Mass introduce us to the first three joyful mysteries of the rosary, three fundamental moments of salvation history, three stages along the way of the Holy Spirit's creative passage through human history: the annunciation, the visitation and the birth of Jesus. In the first reading, St. Paul writes to the Galatians: "But when the designated time had come, God sent forth his Son born of a woman" (4:4). In these few words St. Paul tells us what St. Luke describes at greater length in the Gospel: the visit of the archangel Gabriel to a virgin named Mary, in the town of Nazareth in Galilee. He invites her to become the mother of the Redeemer. The Gospel tells us not only that Mary was surprised and confused by the words of the angel, but that she was afraid. Yes, Mary was afraid, just as we are often afraid! And the angel said, "Do not fear, Mary. For you have found favor with God" (Lk 1:30). It is the power of the Most High that will come upon you, and by the power of the Holy Spirit you will become the mother of the Son of God (cf. Lk 1:35-37).

If the creative power of God is at work at the moment of conception of every human being, in the annunciation the Spirit accomplished something incomparably greater. In the womb of the Virgin Mary the Spirit created a man, to be born nine months later in Bethlehem, who, from the first moment of his conception, was the eternal Son of the Father, the Word through whom all things visible and invisible were made (cf. Jn 1:3)—eternal wisdom, the archetype of everything that exists in creation.

When Mary realized who it was that was calling her, all fear was banished and she replied: "I am the servant of the Lord. Let it be done to me as you say" (Lk 1:38). At that instant, she became the mother of the Son of God. This is the extraordinary truth that we meditate on in the first mystery of the rosary, the annunciation.

All this happened so that, as St. Paul says, we might be redeemed and might receive adoption as God's sons and daughters (cf. Gal 4:5). In Christ, the Holy Spirit makes us God's beloved children. The Incarnation of the Son of God happened once, and is unrepeatable. Divine adoption goes on all the time, through the Church, the body of Christ, and particularly through the sacraments, through baptism, penance, the Eucharist, and of course the sacrament of Pentecost that we call confirmation. Then St. Paul writes something very striking: the proof that we are God's children is that he "has sent forth into our hearts the Spirit of his Son, which cries out 'Abba!' ('Father!')" (Gal 4:6). Abba! Father! This is our prayer every time we say the Our Father. But we have to say it in the Spirit, with a clear awareness that in Christ "we are no longer slaves but children, and therefore heirs with Christ to his kingdom" (cf. Gal 4:7). This new condition of ours as Christians, that is, our transformation through grace and our sharing in divine life itself, will reach its fulfillment in eternity. Then we shall share the happiness with which God himself is happy, Father, Son and Holy Spirit. Do you see how important it is to invoke the Holy Spirit and to allow him to work in us? We must remember that the Holy Spirit can do great things for us! And the Holy Spirit does great things for us every day.

This new condition of ours as Christians, that is, our transformation through grace and our sharing in divine life itself, will reach its fulfillment in eternity.

[Spoken in Spanish]: The next stage of the Holy Spirit's passage is the joyful mystery of the visitation. Moved by the Holy Spirit, who banished her fear, and filled with love for her cousin Elizabeth, who was an older woman and pregnant, Mary immediately left the security of her own home and went to help Elizabeth. Imagine Mary's surprise to hear her cousin say, "But who am I that the mother of my Lord should come to me? The moment your greeting sounded in my ears, the baby leapt for joy" (Lk 1:43-44). That infant was John the Baptist, the greatest of the prophets, the one who would proclaim Jesus at the beginning of his public life.

Then Mary uttered the words of the beautiful hymn of gratitude and praise, the Magnificat: "My being proclaims the greatness of the Lord, my spirit finds joy in God my savior" (Lk 1:46-47). Down the ages the Church repeats the Magnificat every day in what we call the Liturgy of the Hours. Perhaps the most important words of this wonderful hymn are: "God who is mighty has done great things for me, and holy is his name" (Lk 1:49).

Like Mary, you must not be afraid to allow the Holy Spirit to help you become intimate friends of Christ. Like Mary, you must put aside any fear, in order to take Christ to the world in whatever you do—in marriage, as single people in the world, as students, as workers, as professional people. Christ wants to go to many places in the world, and to enter many hearts, through you. Just as Mary visited Elizabeth, so you too are called to "visit" the needs of the poor, the hungry, the homeless, those who are alone or ill, for example, those suffering from AIDS. You are called to stand up for life! To respect and defend the mystery of life always and everywhere, including the lives of unborn babies, giving real help and encouragement to mothers in difficult situations. You are called to work and pray against abortion, against violence of all kinds, including the violence done against women's and children's dignity through pornography. Stand up for the life of the aged and the handicapped, against attempts to promote assisted suicide and euthanasia! Stand up for marriage and family life! Stand up for purity! Resist the pressures and temptations of a world that too often tries to ignore a most fundamental truth: that every life is a gift from God our Creator, and that we must give an account to God of how we use it either for good or evil.

There is yet another stage of the Holy Spirit's passage through history which we should meditate on: the third joyful mystery of the rosary, the birth of the Son of

God, announced by angels to the shepherds. "You have nothing to fear.... This day in David's city a Savior has been born to you.... In a manger you will find an infant wrapped in swaddling clothes" (Lk 2:10-12). St. Luke tells us that the shepherds said to one another: "Let us go over and see this child" (cf. Lk 2:15). And they went and found the child with Mary and Joseph. That is what we too must do! We must go to this child, this man, the Son of God, at whatever inconvenience, at whatever risk to ourselves, because to know and love him will truly change our lives.

You are called to stand up for life!

I remember a song I used to sing in Poland as a young man, a song which I still sing as Pope, which tells about the birth of the Savior. On Christmas night, in every church and chapel, this song would ring out, repeating in a musical way the story told in the Gospel. It says: "In the silence of the night, a voice is heard: 'Get up, shepherds, God is born for you! Hurry to Bethlehem to meet the Lord.'" The same story is told in the beautiful hymn, "Silent Night," which everyone knows. That is a hymn which moves us deeply by reminding us that Jesus, the Son of God, was born of Mary, born to make us holy and to make us adopted sons and daughters of God. It is a hymn to the creative power of the Holy Spirit. It is a song to help us not to be afraid.

If I speak of Christmas, it is because in less than five years we shall reach the end of the second millennium, 2,000 years since the birth of Christ on that first Christmas night in Bethlehem. We must allow the Holy Spirit to prepare us for this important event, which is another significant stage of his passage through history and of our pilgrimage of faith.

Your archbishop, Cardinal O'Connor, has given me the welcome news that the Church in New York will begin to prepare for the millennium by declaring 1996 a year of evangelization. What a wonderful beginning, to make a mighty yearlong effort to transmit the teaching and the love of Christ to all who will listen, especially to those who, for some reason, may have wandered away or have been alienated from the Church. Cardinal O'Connor will need all of you, and especially you young people, to help the Church enter the third millennium. You young people will live most of your lives in the next millennium. You must help the Holy Spirit to shape its social, moral and spiritual character. You must transmit your joy in being adopted sons and daughters of God through the creative power of the Holy Spirit. Do this with the help of Mary, mother of Jesus. Cling to her rosary, and you will never wander far from her side.

The Pope asks you to do this. He knows that you will do this, and for this he loves you. Then you can tell the whole world that you gave the Pope his Christmas present in October, in New York, in Central Park. Do not be afraid! The power of the Holy Spirit is with you!

Come, Holy Spirit, fill the hearts of your faithful! Enkindle in them the fire of your love! Amen.

St. Patrick's Cathedral

Address after the recitation of the rosary in St. Patrick's Cathedral, New York City, October 7, 1995

Dear Cardinal O'Connor, dear brothers and sisters, and distinguished guests,

It is a great joy for me to be here once more in St. Patrick's Cathedral, which is a kind of spiritual landmark for all New Yorkers and, in a sense, for all Catholics in the United States.

From this "house of God," I greet the "household of God in the Spirit" (cf. Eph 2:19): all who have been given "a new birth...unto hope which draws its life from the resurrection of Jesus Christ" (1 Pet 1:3). In the first place I hail my dear friend Cardinal O'Connor, the shepherd of this huge archdiocese, whose dauntless leadership you all know. I greet all of you who have prayed the rosary with me here today on the very feast of the Holy Rosary, especially the sick and the handicapped. I offer respectful greetings as well to the civil authorities of city, state and nation.

I am pleased that Cardinal O'Connor has invited two very special categories of people to pray together this afternoon: representatives of the religious institutes in the archdiocese, and families from every one of the over 400 parishes. These vocations complement each other. The family, the typical lay vocation, witnesses to God's presence in history, through the mutual love of the spouses and their service to life. Religious, living the radical consecration of the evangelical counsels, bear witness that God is absolute and that his kingdom of justice, peace and love is our supreme destiny. Both vocations therefore play an essential part in the Church's mission and in the great enterprise of humanizing the world.

Dear religious, by following Christ along the "narrow and hard way" (cf. Mt 7:14), you experience how true it is that "with him is plenteous redemption": *copiosa apud eum redemptio* (Ps 130:7). For some of you, perhaps, this has been a cross made heavy by temptations to doubt the meaning and purpose of your witness, by attacks on the religious life and on the Church herself. But your fidelity has withstood the challenges from within and without, and remains a singular example to a world so much in need of the "newness of life in Christ" (cf. Rom 6:4) which is made present through the self-giving love that inspires your entire lives (cf. *Perfectae Caritatis,* n. 1).

Every day in my prayer I praise and thank the Father of mercies for the heroic efforts of so many women and men religious who live by "the law of the Spirit, the Spirit of life in Christ Jesus" (Rom 8:2). We must beseech God that, by his grace and through the intercession of Mary and your holy founders and foundresses, a new Pentecost will take hold in consecrated life so that it will become clear to everyone, especially the young, that religious life is a vital, necessary force in the Church. To each one of you and to all the faithful religious of the United States, in words taken from the Letter to the Hebrews I say: "Do not, then, surrender your confidence; it will have great reward" (Heb 10:35). Society needs your prophetic and unmistakable testimony of God's closeness.

We must beseech God that...a new Pentecost will take hold in consecrated life so that it will become clear to everyone, especially the young, that religious life is a vital, necessary force in the Church.

Dear families, dear mothers, fathers, daughters, sons, brothers, sisters, grandparents: I was supposed to come to New York last year for the celebration of the United Nations' Year of the Family. In the letter to families which I wrote on that occasion, I indicated that "the family is placed at the center of the great struggle between good and evil, between life and death, between love and all that is opposed to love" (n. 23). The family therefore is at the heart of the Church's mission and of her concern for humanity.

When a man and a woman bind themselves to each other without reservation in their decision to be faithful "in sickness and in health, in good times and in bad," to the exclusion of every other physical love, they become cooperators with the Creator in bringing new life into the world. You parents can look with love at your children and say: this is "flesh of my flesh" (Gen 2:23). Your life is defined by your fatherly and motherly desire and duty to give your children the best: a loving home, an upbringing, a healthy and positive start on the road of life, now and for eternity. Above all, through baptism you make it possible for your children to become God's beloved sons and daughters, mystically united with Christ, incorporated into his Church! Consider how important it is for you to foster the life of faith and the life of grace in yourselves and in your children. Beneath the high altar of this cathedral, together with the former cardinals and archbishops of New York, there is buried the Servant of God Pierre Toussaint, a married man, a one-time slave from Haiti. What is so extraordinary about this man? He radiated a most serene and joyful faith, nourished daily by the Eucharist and visits to the Blessed Sacrament. In the face of constant, painful discrimination he understood, as few have understood, the meaning of the words: "Father, forgive them; they do not know what they are doing" (Lk 23:34). No treasure is as uplifting and transforming as the light of faith.

From many points of view, these are difficult times for parents who wish to pass on to their children the treasure of the Catholic faith. Sometimes you yourselves are not sure what the Church stands for. There are false teachers and dissenting voices. Bad examples cause great harm. Furthermore, a self-indulgent culture undermines many of the values which are at the basis of sound family life.

There are two immediate things which the Catholic families of America can do to strengthen home life. The first is prayer: both personal and family prayer. Prayer raises our minds and hearts to God to thank him for his blessings, to ask him for his help. It brings the saving power of Jesus Christ into the decisions and actions of everyday life.

There are two immediate things which the Catholic families of America can do to strengthen home life. The first is prayer: both personal and family prayer.

One prayer in particular I recommend to families: the one we have just been praying, the rosary, and especially the joyful mysteries, which help us to meditate on the Holy Family of Nazareth. Uniting her will with the will of God, Mary conceived the Christ Child, and became the model of every mother carrying her unborn child. By visiting her cousin Elizabeth, Mary took to another family the healing presence of Jesus. Mary gave birth to the infant Jesus in the humblest of circumstances and presented him to Simeon in the temple, as every baby may be presented to God in baptism. Mary and Joseph worried over the lost child before they found him in the temple, so that parents of all generations would know that the trials and sorrows of family life are the road to closer union with Jesus. To use a phrase made famous by the late Father Patrick Peyton: The family that prays together, stays together!

The second suggestion I make to families is to use the *Catechism of the Catholic Church* to learn about the faith and to answer the questions that come up, especially the moral questions which confront everyone today. Dear parents, you are educators because you are parents. I exhort and encourage the bishops and the whole Church in the United States to help parents to fulfill their vocation to be the first and most important teachers of the faith to their children. And I wish to say a special word of thanks to all those who make sacrifices, sometimes heroic sacrifices, to ensure that Catholic children receive formation in the faith either through the Catholic school system or through religious education programs in your parishes. I know that the Archdiocese of New York is proud of its Catholic schools and its religious education programs. Immense effort goes into these undertakings, in the face of great odds. May God reward everyone involved!

The second suggestion I make to families is to use the Catechism of the Catholic Church *to learn about the faith and to answer the questions that come up, especially the moral questions which confront everyone today.*

Families in difficulties or couples in irregular situations also have a claim on the Church's pastoral care. Other stronger and spiritually mature families can play a wonderful role in bringing encouragement and help to such couples and families. Every strengthening of family bonds is a victory for society. I appeal to all of you to promote respect for the mystery of life and love which God has entrusted in a special way to families.

And to religious, I appeal to you to be, in the heart of the Church in the United States, what the Second Vatican Council called you: "a blazing emblem of the heavenly kingdom" *(Perfectae Caritatis,* n. 1).

God bless you all!

God bless the Church in New York!

The Vatican Mission to the U.N.

An address given when the Pope blessed the offices of the Permanent Observer Mission of the Holy See to the United Nations, New York, October 7, 1995

My dear brothers and sisters,

As the third millennium approaches, we are given an opportunity to reflect on the Lord's power and presence in our lives and in our world. Nearly 2,000 years ago Jesus Christ ushered in the kingdom of God here on earth, and in our own time he continues to draw men and women to the light of his truth. Just as he commanded his Church in her earliest days to "make disciples of all the nations" (Mt 28:19), so he calls the faithful today, bishops, priests, religious and laity alike, to be instruments of evangelization for the salvation of the entire human family.

It is ultimately for this reason that, over thirty years ago, Pope Paul VI initiated the formal participation of the Holy See in the United Nations organization, offering the cooperation of the Church's spiritual and humanitarian expertise to the men and women of good will who work for the advancement of peace and justice in the international community. In this capacity, the Holy See continues to remind the nations that their focal point must always be the integral good of the human person.

Nearly 2,000 years ago Jesus Christ ushered in the kingdom of God here on earth, and in our own time he continues to draw men and women to the light of his truth.

With the intention of expanding this activity beyond the strictly diplomatic parameters of the Holy See's mission to the United Nations organization, the Path to Peace Foundation was established in 1991. Since then, the foundation has borne much fruit in spreading the message by which the Catholic Church, through the ministry of the successor of Peter and the activities of the Holy See, strives to "guide our feet into the way of peace" (Lk 1:79).

Every year, the Path to Peace Foundation pays tribute to a single individual for his or her outstanding service to the cause of world peace, and acknowledges those often unsung heroes in many fields, whose sole purpose and desire is to be present where needs are greatest. It likewise recognizes men and women who give of their time, talents and resources in order to provide the means to sustain and expand the Church's evangelical mission of making Christ known to the ends of the earth.

This newly acquired facility is a testimony to the support and commitment of so many people both to the Holy See's mission and to the Path to Peace Foundation in their joint work for world peace. To all of you, benefactors and volunteers, I express my heartfelt gratitude. As we dedicate this building to the cause of Christ, let us rededicate ourselves to his service, working and praying always for the salvation of the whole human family.

Oriole Park

A homily given at a Mass at Oriole Park at Camden Yards in Baltimore, Maryland, October 8, 1995

"Oh, that today you would hear his voice:
harden not your hearts" (Ps 95:7-8).

Dear brothers and sisters in Christ,

Each day, the Church begins the Liturgy of the Hours with the psalm which we have just prayed together: "Come, let us sing joyfully to the Lord!" (Ps 95:1). In that call, ringing down the centuries and echoing across the face of the globe, the psalmist summons the people of God to sing the praises of the Lord and to bear great witness to the marvelous things God has done for us. Priests, women and men religious, and increasing numbers of lay people daily recite the Liturgy of the Hours, giving rise to a powerful mobilization of praise to God—*officium laudis*—to God who, through his word, created the world and all that is in it: "In his hands are the depths of the earth, and the tops of the mountains are his. His is the sea, for he has made it, and the dry land, which his hands have formed" (Ps 95:4-5).

Not only are we God's creatures. In his infinite mercy, God has chosen us as his beloved people: "For he is our God, and we are the people he shepherds, the flock he guides" (Ps 95:7). He chose us in Christ, the Good Shepherd, who gave his life for his sheep and who calls us to the banquet of his Body and Blood, the holy Eucharist which we are celebrating together this morning.

The psalmist's call to hear the Lord's voice has particular significance for us as we celebrate this Mass in Baltimore. Maryland was the birthplace of the Church in colonial America. More than 360 years ago, a small band of Catholics came to the New World to build a home where they could "sing joyfully to the Lord" (Ps 95:1) in freedom. They established a colony whose hallmark was religious tolerance, which would later become one of the cultural cornerstones of American democracy. Baltimore is the senior metropolitan see in the United States. Its first bishop, John Carroll, stands out as a model who can still inspire the Church in America today. Here were held the great provincial and plenary councils which guided the Church's expansion as waves of immigrants came to these shores in search of a better life. Here in Baltimore, in 1884, the Bishops of the United States authorized the *Baltimore Catechism*, which formed the faith of tens of millions of Catholics for decades. In Baltimore, the country's Catholic school system began under the leadership of St. Elizabeth Ann Seton. The first seminary in the United States was established here, under the protection of the Virgin Mother of God, as was America's first Catholic college for women. Since those heroic beginnings, men and women of every race and social class have built the Catholic community we see in America today, a great spiritual movement of witness, of apostolate, of good works, of Catholic institutions and organizations.

The challenge of the great jubilee of the year 2000 is the new evangelization: a deepening of faith and a vigorous response to the Christian vocation to holiness and service.

With warm affection therefore I greet your archbishop, Cardinal Keeler, and thank him for his sensitive leadership in this local Church and his work on behalf of the bishops' conference. With esteem I greet the other cardinals and bishops present here in great numbers, the priests, deacons and seminarians, the women and men religious, and all God's people, the "living stones" (1 Pet 2:5) whom the Spirit uses to build up the Body of Christ. I gladly greet the members of the various Christian Churches and ecclesial communities. I assure them of the Catholic Church's ardent desire to celebrate the Jubilee of the Year 2000 as a great occasion to move closer to overcoming the divisions of the second millennium (cf. *Tertio Millennio Adveniente,* n. 34). I thank the civil authorities who have wished to share this sacred moment with us.

[Spoken in Spanish]: I greet the Spanish-speaking faithful present here and all those following this Mass on radio or television. The Church is your spiritual home. Your parishes, associations, schools and religious education programs need your cooperation and the enthusiasm of your faith. With special affection, I encourage you to transmit your Catholic traditions to the younger generations.

Our celebration today speaks to us not only of the past. The Eucharist always makes present anew the saving mystery of Christ's death and resurrection, and points to the future definitive fulfillment of God's plan of salvation. Two years ago, at Denver, I was deeply impressed by the vitality of America's young people as they bore enthusiastic witness to their love of Christ, and showed that they were not afraid of the demands of the Gospel. Today, I offer this Mass for a strengthening of that vitality and Christian courage at every level of the Church in the United States: among the laity, among the priests and religious, among my brother bishops. The whole Church is preparing for the third Christian millennium. The challenge of the great jubilee of the year 2000 is the new evangelization: a deepening of faith and a vigorous response to the Christian vocation to holiness and service. This is what the successor of Peter has come to Baltimore to urge upon each one of you: the courage to bear witness to the Gospel of our redemption.

In today's Gospel reading, the apostles ask Jesus: "Increase our faith" (Lk 17:5). This must be our constant prayer. Faith is always demanding, because faith leads us beyond ourselves. It leads us directly to God. Faith also imparts a vision of life's purpose and stimulates us to action. The Gospel of Jesus Christ is not a private opinion, a remote spiritual ideal, or a mere program for personal growth. The Gospel is the power which can transform the world! The Gospel is no abstraction: it is the living person of Jesus Christ, the Word of God, the reflection of the Father's glory (cf. Heb 1:2), the Incarnate Son who reveals the deepest meaning of our humanity and the noble destiny to which the whole human family is called (cf. *Gaudium et Spes*, n. 22). Christ has commanded us to let the light of the Gospel shine forth in our service to society. How can we profess faith in God's word, and then refuse to let it inspire and direct our thinking, our activity, our decisions, and our responsibilities toward one another?

The Gospel is the power which can transform the world!

In America, Christian faith has found expression in an impressive array of witnesses and achievements. We must recall with gratitude the inspiring work of education carried out in countless families, schools and universities, and all the healing and consolation imparted in hospitals and hospices and shelters. We must give thanks for the practical living out of God's call in devoted service to others, in commitment to social justice, in responsible involvement in political life, in a wide variety of charitable and social organizations, and in the growth of ecumenical and interreligious understanding and cooperation. In a more global context, we should thank God for the great generosity of American Catholics whose support of the foreign missions has greatly contributed to the spiritual and material well-being of their brothers and sisters in other lands. The Church in the United States has sent brave missionary men and women out to the nations, and not a few of them have borne the ultimate witness to the ancient truth that the blood of martyrs is the seed of Christianity. In my visits to Catholic communities around the world I often meet American missionaries, lay, religious and priests. I wish to make an appeal to young Catholics to consider the missionary vocation. I know that the "spirit of Denver" is alive in many young hearts. Christ needs many more committed men and women to take that "spirit" to the four corners of the world.

Today though, some Catholics are tempted to discouragement or disillusionment, like the prophet Habakkuk in the first reading. They are tempted to cry out to the Lord in a different way. Why does God not intervene when violence threatens his people? Why does God let us see ruin and misery? Why does God permit evil? Like the prophet Habakkuk, and like the thirsty Israelites in the desert at Meribah and Massah, our trust can falter; we can lose patience with God. In the drama of history, we can find our dependence upon God burdensome rather than liberating. We too can "harden our hearts."

And yet the prophet gives us an answer to our impatience: "If God delays, wait for him; he will surely come, he will not be late" (cf. Heb 2:3). A Polish proverb expresses the same conviction in another way: "God takes his time, but he is just." Our waiting for God is never in vain. Every moment is our opportunity to model ourselves on Jesus Christ—to allow the power of the Gospel to transform our personal lives and our service to others, according to the spirit of the Beatitudes. "Bear your share of the hardship which the Gospel entails," writes Paul to Timothy in today's second reading (2 Tim 1:8). This is no idle exhortation to endurance. No, it is an invitation to enter more deeply into the Christian vocation which belongs to us all by baptism. There is no evil to be faced that Christ does not face with us. There is no enemy that Christ has not already conquered. There is no cross to bear that Christ has not already borne for us, and does not now bear with us. And on the far side of every cross we find the newness of life in the Holy Spirit, that new life which will reach its fulfillment in the resurrection. This is our faith. This is our witness before the world.

I wish to make an appeal to young Catholics to consider the missionary vocation.

Dear brothers and sisters in Christ: openness to the Lord—a willingness to let the Lord transform our lives—should produce a renewed spiritual and missionary vitality among American Catholics. Jesus Christ is the answer to the question posed by every human life, and the love of Christ compels us to share that great good news with everyone. We believe that the death and resurrection of Christ reveal the true meaning of human existence; therefore nothing that is genuinely human fails to find an echo in our hearts. Christ died for all, so we must be at the service of all. "The Spirit God has given us is no cowardly spirit.... Therefore, never be ashamed of your testimony to our Lord" (2 Tim 1:7-8). Thus wrote St. Paul to Timothy, almost 2,000 years ago; thus speaks the Church to American Catholics today.

Jesus Christ is the answer to the question posed by every human life, and the love of Christ compels us to share that great good news with everyone.

Christian witness takes different forms at different moments in the life of a nation. Sometimes, witnessing to Christ will mean drawing out of a culture the full meaning of its noblest intentions, a fullness that is revealed in Christ. At other times, witnessing to Christ means challenging that culture, especially when the truth about the human person is under assault. America has always wanted to be a land of the free. Today, the challenge facing America is to find freedom's fulfillment in the truth—the truth that is intrinsic to human life created in God's image and likeness, the truth that is written on the human heart, the truth that can be known by reason and can therefore form the basis of a profound and universal dialogue among people about the direction they must give to their lives and their activities.

One hundred thirty years ago, President Abraham Lincoln asked whether a nation "conceived in liberty and dedicated to the proposition that all men are created equal" could "long endure." President Lincoln's question is no less a question for the present generation of Americans. Democracy cannot be sustained without a shared commitment to certain moral truths about the human person and human community. The basic question before a democratic society is: "how ought we to live together?" In seeking an answer to this question, can society exclude moral truth and moral reasoning? Can the biblical wisdom which played such a formative part in the very founding of your country be excluded from that debate? Would not doing so mean that America's founding documents no longer have any defining content, but are only the formal dressing of changing opinion? Would not doing so mean that tens of millions of Americans could no longer offer the contribution of their deepest convictions to the formation of public policy? Surely it is important for America that the moral truths which make freedom possible should be passed on to each new generation. Every generation of Americans needs to know that freedom consists not in doing what we like, but in having the right to do what we ought.

How appropriate is St. Paul's charge to Timothy! "Guard the rich deposit of faith with the help of the Holy Spirit who dwells within us" (2 Tim 1:14). That charge speaks to parents and teachers; it speaks in a special and urgent way to you, my brother bishops, successors of the apostles. Christ asks us to guard the truth because, as he promised us: "You will know the truth and the truth will make you free" (Jn 8:32). *Depositum custodi!* We must guard the truth that is the condition of authentic freedom, the truth that allows freedom to be fulfilled in goodness. We must guard the deposit of divine truth handed down to us in the Church, especially in view of the challenges posed by a materialistic culture and by a permissive mentality that reduces freedom to license. But we bishops must do more than guard this truth. We must proclaim it, in season and out of season; we must celebrate it with God's people, in the sacraments; we must live it in charity and service; we must bear public witness to the truth that is Jesus Christ.

Every generation of Americans needs to know that freedom consists not in doing what we like, but in having the right to do what we ought.

Catholics of America! Always be guided by the truth—by the truth about God who created and redeemed us, and by the truth about the human person, made in the image and likeness of God and destined for a glorious fulfillment in the kingdom to come. Always be convincing witnesses to the truth. "Stir into a flame the gift of God" that has been bestowed upon you in baptism. Light your nation—light the world—with the power of that flame! Amen.

Departure from Baltimore-Washington International Airport

Farewell remarks as the Pope returned to Rome, October 8, 1995

Dear Mr. Vice President, dear friends,
dear people of America,

As I take leave of the United States, I wish to express my deep and abiding gratitude to many people.

To you, Mr. Vice President, for graciously coming here to say goodbye. To the bishops of the dioceses I have visited and the many people who have worked so hard to make this visit a success. To the public authorities, to the police and security personnel who have ensured efficiency, good order and safety.

To the representatives of the various churches and ecclesial communities who have received me with great good will; to Americans of all races, colors and creeds who have followed with interest and attention the events of these days; to the men and women of the communications media, who have labored diligently to bring the words and images of this visit to millions of people; and especially to all those who, personally present or from afar, have supported me with their prayers.

I express to the Catholic community of the United States my heartfelt thanks. In the words of St. Paul: "I give thanks to my God every time I think of you—which is constantly in every prayer I utter."

I say to you again, America, in the light of your own tradition: love life, cherish life, defend life, from conception to natural death.

I say this too, to the United States of America: today, in our world as it is, many other nations and peoples look to you as the principal model and pattern for their own advancement in democracy. But democracy needs wisdom. Democracy needs virtues, if it is not to turn against everything that it is meant to defend and encourage. Democracy stands or falls with the truths and values which it embodies and promotes.

Democracy serves what is true and right when it safeguards the dignity of every human person, when it respects inviolable and inalienable human rights, when it makes the common good the end and criterion regulating all public and social life. But these values themselves must have an objective content. Otherwise they correspond only to the power of the majority, or the wishes of the most vocal. If an attitude of skepticism were to succeed in calling into question even the fundamental principles of the moral law, the democratic system itself would be shaken in its foundations.

The United States possesses a safeguard, a great bulwark, against this happening. I speak of your founding documents: the Declaration of Independence, the Constitution, the Bill of Rights. These documents are grounded in and embody unchanging principles of the natural law whose permanent truth and validity can be known by reason, for it is the law written by God in human hearts.

At the center of the moral vision of your founding documents is the recognition of the rights of the human person, and especially respect for the dignity and sanctity of human life in all conditions and at all stages of development. I say to you again, America, in the light of your own tradition: love life, cherish life, defend life, from conception to natural death.

At the end of your National Anthem, one finds these words:

> "Then conquer we must, when our cause it is just,
> And this be our motto: 'In God is our trust!'"

America: may your trust always be in God and in none other. Then:

> "The star-spangled banner in triumph shall wave
> O'er the land of the free and the home of the brave."

Thank you, and God bless you all. Thank you very much.

St. Paul Book & Media Centers

ALASKA
750 West 5th Ave., Anchorage, AK 99501; 907-272-8183

CALIFORNIA
3908 Sepulveda Blvd., Culver City, CA 90230; 310-397-8676
5945 Balboa Ave., San Diego, CA 92111; 619-565-9181
46 Geary Street, San Francisco, CA 94108; 415-781-5180

FLORIDA
145 S.W. 107th Ave., Miami, FL 33174; 305-559-6715

HAWAII
1143 Bishop Street, Honolulu, HI 96813; 808-521-2731

ILLINOIS
172 North Michigan Ave., Chicago, IL 60601; 312-346-4228

LOUISIANA
4403 Veterans Memorial Blvd., Metairie, LA 70006; 504-887-7631

MASSACHUSETTS
50 St. Paul's Ave., Jamaica Plain, Boston, MA 02130; 617-522-8911
Rte. 1, 885 Providence Hwy., Dedham, MA 02026; 617-326-5385

MISSOURI
9804 Watson Rd., St. Louis, MO 63126; 314-965-3512

NEW JERSEY
561 U.S. Route 1, Wick Plaza, Edison, NJ 08817; 908-572-1200

NEW YORK
150 East 52nd Street, New York, NY 10022; 212-754-1110
78 Fort Place, Staten Island, NY 10301; 718-447-5071

OHIO
2105 Ontario Street, Cleveland, OH 44115; 216-621-9427

PENNSYLVANIA
Northeast Shopping Center, 9171-A Roosevelt Blvd. (between Grant Ave.
& Welsh Rd.), Philadelphia, PA 19114; 610-277-7728

SOUTH CAROLINA
243 King Street, Charleston, SC 29401; 803-577-0175

TENNESSEE
4811 Poplar Ave., Memphis, TN 38117; 901-761-2987

TEXAS
114 Main Plaza, San Antonio, TX 78205; 210-224-8101

VIRGINIA
1025 King Street, Alexandria, VA 22314; 703-549-3806

GUAM
285 Farenholt Ave., Suite 308, Tamuning, Guam 96911; 671-649-4377

CANADA
3022 Dufferin Street, Toronto, Ontario, Canada M6B 3T5; 416-781-9131